ADDRESS BOOK

This Book Belongs To:

PHONE BOOK

Name	Phone

PHONE BOOK

Name	**Phone**

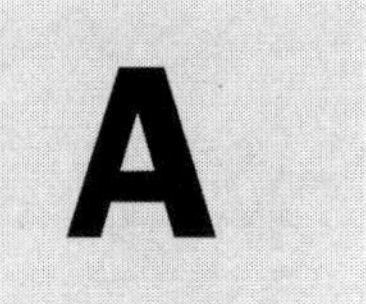

ADDRESS LOG

NAME :

Address :

Email :

Home :

Work :

Phone :

Social Media :

Birthday :

• •

NAME :

Address :

Email :

Home :

Work :

Phone :

Social Media :

Birthday :

• •

NAME :

Address :

Email :

Home :

Work :

Phone :

Social Media :

Birthday :

ADDRESS LOG

NAME :

Address :

Email :

Home :

Work :

Phone :

Social Media :

Birthday :

• •

NAME :

Address :

Email :

Home :

Work :

Phone :

Social Media :

Birthday :

• •

NAME :

Address :

Email :

Home :

Work :

Phone :

Social Media :

Birthday :

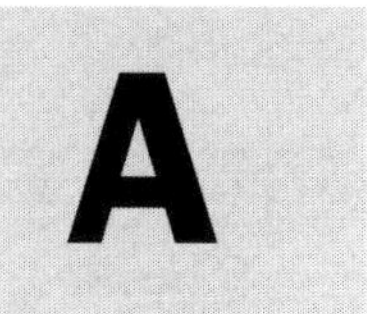

ADDRESS LOG

NAME :

Address :

Email :

Home :

Work :

Phone :

Social Media :

Birthday :

• •

NAME :

Address :

Email :

Home :

Work :

Phone :

Social Media :

Birthday :

• •

NAME :

Address :

Email :

Home :

Work :

Phone :

Social Media :

Birthday :

ADDRESS LOG

NAME :

Address :

Email :

Home :

Work :

Phone :

Social Media :

Birthday :

• •

NAME :

Address :

Email :

Home :

Work :

Phone :

Social Media :

Birthday :

• •

NAME :

Address :

Email :

Home :

Work :

Phone :

Social Media :

Birthday :

ADDRESS LOG

NAME :

Address :

Email :

Home :

Work :

Phone :

Social Media :

Birthday :

• •

NAME :

Address :

Email :

Home :

Work :

Phone :

Social Media :

Birthday :

• •

NAME :

Address :

Email :

Home :

Work :

Phone :

Social Media :

Birthday :

ADDRESS LOG

NAME : ______________________

Address : ______________________

Email : ______________________

Home : ______________________

Work : ______________________

Phone : ______________________

Social Media : ______________________

Birthday : ______________________

• •

NAME : ______________________

Address : ______________________

Email : ______________________

Home : ______________________

Work : ______________________

Phone : ______________________

Social Media : ______________________

Birthday : ______________________

• •

NAME : ______________________

Address : ______________________

Email : ______________________

Home : ______________________

Work : ______________________

Phone : ______________________

Social Media : ______________________

Birthday : ______________________

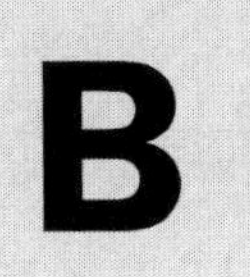

ADDRESS LOG

NAME : ____________________

Address : ____________________

Email : ____________________

Home : ____________________

Work : ____________________

Phone : ____________________

Social Media : ____________________

Birthday : ____________________

• •

NAME : ____________________

Address : ____________________

Email : ____________________

Home : ____________________

Work : ____________________

Phone : ____________________

Social Media : ____________________

Birthday : ____________________

• •

NAME : ____________________

Address : ____________________

Email : ____________________

Home : ____________________

Work : ____________________

Phone : ____________________

Social Media : ____________________

Birthday : ____________________

ADDRESS LOG

B

NAME :

Address :

Email :

Home :

Work :

Phone :

Social Media :

Birthday :

• •

NAME :

Address :

Email :

Home :

Work :

Phone :

Social Media :

Birthday :

• •

NAME :

Address :

Email :

Home :

Work :

Phone :

Social Media :

Birthday :

ADDRESS LOG

NAME :

Address :

Email :

Home :

Work :

Phone :

Social Media :

Birthday :

• •

NAME :

Address :

Email :

Home :

Work :

Phone :

Social Media :

Birthday :

• •

NAME :

Address :

Email :

Home :

Work :

Phone :

Social Media :

Birthday :

ADDRESS LOG

C

NAME :

Address :

Email :

Home :

Work :

Phone :

Social Media :

Birthday :

NAME :

Address :

Email :

Home :

Work :

Phone :

Social Media :

Birthday :

NAME :

Address :

Email :

Home :

Work :

Phone :

Social Media :

Birthday :

ADDRESS LOG

NAME :

Address :

Email :

Home :

Work :

Phone :

Social Media :

Birthday :

• •

NAME :

Address :

Email :

Home :

Work :

Phone :

Social Media :

Birthday :

• •

NAME :

Address :

Email :

Home :

Work :

Phone :

Social Media :

Birthday :

ADDRESS LOG

C

NAME :

Address :

Email :

Home :

Work :

Phone :

Social Media :

Birthday :

• •

NAME :

Address :

Email :

Home :

Work :

Phone :

Social Media :

Birthday :

• •

NAME :

Address :

Email :

Home :

Work :

Phone :

Social Media :

Birthday :

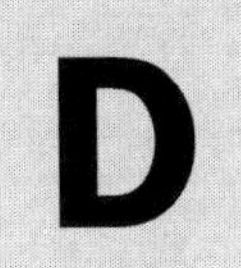

ADDRESS LOG

NAME : ______________________

Address : ______________________

Email : ______________________

Home : ______________________

Work : ______________________

Phone : ______________________

Social Media : ______________________

Birthday : ______________________

• •

NAME : ______________________

Address : ______________________

Email : ______________________

Home : ______________________

Work : ______________________

Phone : ______________________

Social Media : ______________________

Birthday : ______________________

• •

NAME : ______________________

Address : ______________________

Email : ______________________

Home : ______________________

Work : ______________________

Phone : ______________________

Social Media : ______________________

Birthday : ______________________

ADDRESS LOG

NAME :
Address :
Email :
Home :
Work :
Phone :
Social Media :
Birthday :

• •

NAME :
Address :
Email :
Home :
Work :
Phone :
Social Media :
Birthday :

• •

NAME :
Address :
Email :
Home :
Work :
Phone :
Social Media :
Birthday :

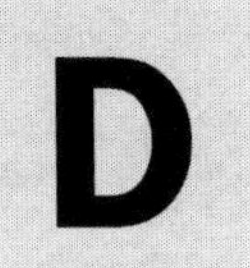

ADDRESS LOG

NAME : ______________________

Address : ______________________

Email : ______________________

Home : ______________________

Work : ______________________

Phone : ______________________

Social Media : ______________________

Birthday : ______________________

• •

NAME : ______________________

Address : ______________________

Email : ______________________

Home : ______________________

Work : ______________________

Phone : ______________________

Social Media : ______________________

Birthday : ______________________

• •

NAME : ______________________

Address : ______________________

Email : ______________________

Home : ______________________

Work : ______________________

Phone : ______________________

Social Media : ______________________

Birthday : ______________________

ADDRESS LOG

NAME :
Address :
Email :
Home :
Work :
Phone :
Social Media :
Birthday :

• •

NAME :
Address :
Email :
Home :
Work :
Phone :
Social Media :
Birthday :

• •

NAME :
Address :
Email :
Home :
Work :
Phone :
Social Media :
Birthday :

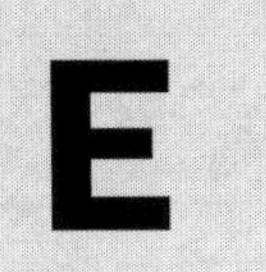

ADDRESS LOG

NAME :

Address :

Email :

Home :

Work :

Phone :

Social Media :

Birthday :

NAME :

Address :

Email :

Home :

Work :

Phone :

Social Media :

Birthday :

NAME :

Address :

Email :

Home :

Work :

Phone :

Social Media :

Birthday :

ADDRESS LOG

NAME :

Address :

Email :

Home :

Work :

Phone :

Social Media :

Birthday :

• •

NAME :

Address :

Email :

Home :

Work :

Phone :

Social Media :

Birthday :

• •

NAME :

Address :

Email :

Home :

Work :

Phone :

Social Media :

Birthday :

ADDRESS LOG

NAME :

Address :

Email :

Home :

Work :

Phone :

Social Media :

Birthday :

• •

NAME :

Address :

Email :

Home :

Work :

Phone :

Social Media :

Birthday :

• •

NAME :

Address :

Email :

Home :

Work :

Phone :

Social Media :

Birthday :

ADDRESS LOG

NAME :

Address :

Email :

Home :

Work :

Phone :

Social Media :

Birthday :

• •

NAME :

Address :

Email :

Home :

Work :

Phone :

Social Media :

Birthday :

• •

NAME :

Address :

Email :

Home :

Work :

Phone :

Social Media :

Birthday :

ADDRESS LOG

NAME :

Address :

Email :

Home :

Work :

Phone :

Social Media :

Birthday :

• •

NAME :

Address :

Email :

Home :

Work :

Phone :

Social Media :

Birthday :

• •

NAME :

Address :

Email :

Home :

Work :

Phone :

Social Media :

Birthday :

ADDRESS LOG

F

NAME :

Address :

Email :

Home :

Work :

Phone :

Social Media :

Birthday :

• •

NAME :

Address :

Email :

Home :

Work :

Phone :

Social Media :

Birthday :

• •

NAME :

Address :

Email :

Home :

Work :

Phone :

Social Media :

Birthday :

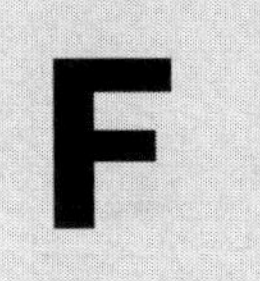

ADDRESS LOG

NAME : ______________________

Address : ______________________

Email : ______________________

Home : ______________________

Work : ______________________

Phone : ______________________

Social Media : ______________________

Birthday : ______________________

• •

NAME : ______________________

Address : ______________________

Email : ______________________

Home : ______________________

Work : ______________________

Phone : ______________________

Social Media : ______________________

Birthday : ______________________

• •

NAME : ______________________

Address : ______________________

Email : ______________________

Home : ______________________

Work : ______________________

Phone : ______________________

Social Media : ______________________

Birthday : ______________________

ADDRESS LOG

F

NAME :
Address :
Email :
Home :
Work :
Phone :
Social Media :
Birthday :

• •

NAME :
Address :
Email :
Home :
Work :
Phone :
Social Media :
Birthday :

• •

NAME :
Address :
Email :
Home :
Work :
Phone :
Social Media :
Birthday :

ADDRESS LOG

NAME :

Address :

Email :

Home :

Work :

Phone :

Social Media :

Birthday :

• •

NAME :

Address :

Email :

Home :

Work :

Phone :

Social Media :

Birthday :

• •

NAME :

Address :

Email :

Home :

Work :

Phone :

Social Media :

Birthday :

ADDRESS LOG

G

NAME : ____________________

Address :

Email :

Home :

Work :

Phone :

Social Media :

Birthday :

• •

NAME : ____________________

Address :

Email :

Home :

Work :

Phone :

Social Media :

Birthday :

• •

NAME : ____________________

Address :

Email :

Home :

Work :

Phone :

Social Media :

Birthday :

G

ADDRESS LOG

NAME :

Address :

Email :

Home :

Work :

Phone :

Social Media :

Birthday :

• •

NAME :

Address :

Email :

Home :

Work :

Phone :

Social Media :

Birthday :

• •

NAME :

Address :

Email :

Home :

Work :

Phone :

Social Media :

Birthday :

ADDRESS LOG

G

NAME :

Address :

Email :

Home :

Work :

Phone :

Social Media :

Birthday :

• •

NAME :

Address :

Email :

Home :

Work :

Phone :

Social Media :

Birthday :

• •

NAME :

Address :

Email :

Home :

Work :

Phone :

Social Media :

Birthday :

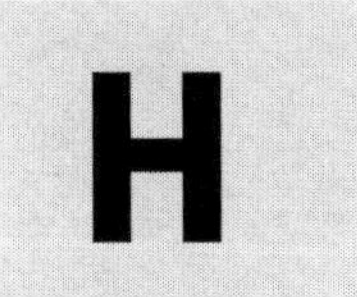

ADDRESS LOG

NAME :

Address :

Email :

Home :

Work :

Phone :

Social Media :

Birthday :

NAME :

Address :

Email :

Home :

Work :

Phone :

Social Media :

Birthday :

NAME :

Address :

Email :

Home :

Work :

Phone :

Social Media :

Birthday :

ADDRESS LOG

NAME :

Address :

Email :

Home :

Work :

Phone :

Social Media :

Birthday :

NAME :

Address :

Email :

Home :

Work :

Phone :

Social Media :

Birthday :

NAME :

Address :

Email :

Home :

Work :

Phone :

Social Media :

Birthday :

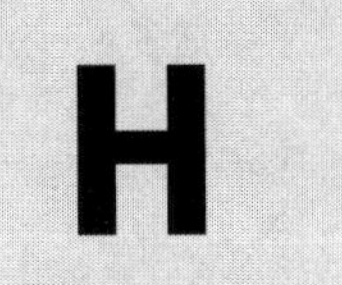

ADDRESS LOG

NAME : ______________________

Address : ______________________

Email : ______________________

Home : ______________________

Work : ______________________

Phone : ______________________

Social Media : ______________________

Birthday : ______________________

• •

NAME : ______________________

Address : ______________________

Email : ______________________

Home : ______________________

Work : ______________________

Phone : ______________________

Social Media : ______________________

Birthday : ______________________

• •

NAME : ______________________

Address : ______________________

Email : ______________________

Home : ______________________

Work : ______________________

Phone : ______________________

Social Media : ______________________

Birthday : ______________________

ADDRESS LOG

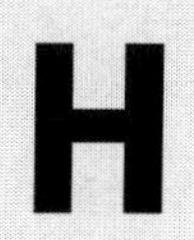

NAME :
Address :
Email :
Home :
Work :
Phone :
Social Media :
Birthday :

• •

NAME :
Address :
Email :
Home :
Work :
Phone :
Social Media :
Birthday :

• •

NAME :
Address :
Email :
Home :
Work :
Phone :
Social Media :
Birthday :

ADDRESS LOG

NAME :

Address :

Email :

Home :

Work :

Phone :

Social Media :

Birthday :

NAME :

Address :

Email :

Home :

Work :

Phone :

Social Media :

Birthday :

NAME :

Address :

Email :

Home :

Work :

Phone :

Social Media :

Birthday :

ADDRESS LOG

I

NAME :
Address :
Email :
Home :
Work :
Phone :
Social Media :
Birthday :

• •

NAME :
Address :
Email :
Home :
Work :
Phone :
Social Media :
Birthday :

• •

NAME :
Address :
Email :
Home :
Work :
Phone :
Social Media :
Birthday :

I

ADDRESS LOG

NAME :

Address :

Email :

Home :

Work :

Phone :

Social Media :

Birthday :

• •

NAME :

Address :

Email :

Home :

Work :

Phone :

Social Media :

Birthday :

• •

NAME :

Address :

Email :

Home :

Work :

Phone :

Social Media :

Birthday :

ADDRESS LOG

I

NAME :

Address :

Email :

Home :

Work :

Phone :

Social Media :

Birthday :

• •

NAME :

Address :

Email :

Home :

Work :

Phone :

Social Media :

Birthday :

• •

NAME :

Address :

Email :

Home :

Work :

Phone :

Social Media :

Birthday :

J

ADDRESS LOG

NAME :

Address :

Email :

Home :

Work :

Phone :

Social Media :

Birthday :

• •

NAME :

Address :

Email :

Home :

Work :

Phone :

Social Media :

Birthday :

• •

NAME :

Address :

Email :

Home :

Work :

Phone :

Social Media :

Birthday :

ADDRESS LOG

J

NAME :

Address :

Email :

Home :

Work :

Phone :

Social Media :

Birthday :

• •

NAME :

Address :

Email :

Home :

Work :

Phone :

Social Media :

Birthday :

• •

NAME :

Address :

Email :

Home :

Work :

Phone :

Social Media :

Birthday :

J

ADDRESS LOG

NAME :

Address :

Email :

Home :

Work :

Phone :

Social Media :

Birthday :

• •

NAME :

Address :

Email :

Home :

Work :

Phone :

Social Media :

Birthday :

• •

NAME :

Address :

Email :

Home :

Work :

Phone :

Social Media :

Birthday :

ADDRESS LOG

J

NAME :
Address :
Email :
Home :
Work :
Phone :
Social Media :
Birthday :

NAME :
Address :
Email :
Home :
Work :
Phone :
Social Media :
Birthday :

NAME :
Address :
Email :
Home :
Work :
Phone :
Social Media :
Birthday :

ADDRESS LOG

NAME :

Address :

Email :

Home :

Work :

Phone :

Social Media :

Birthday :

• •

NAME :

Address :

Email :

Home :

Work :

Phone :

Social Media :

Birthday :

• •

NAME :

Address :

Email :

Home :

Work :

Phone :

Social Media :

Birthday :

ADDRESS LOG

NAME :

Address :

Email :

Home :

Work :

Phone :

Social Media :

Birthday :

• •

NAME :

Address :

Email :

Home :

Work :

Phone :

Social Media :

Birthday :

• •

NAME :

Address :

Email :

Home :

Work :

Phone :

Social Media :

Birthday :

ADDRESS LOG

NAME :

Address :

Email :

Home :

Work :

Phone :

Social Media :

Birthday :

NAME :

Address :

Email :

Home :

Work :

Phone :

Social Media :

Birthday :

NAME :

Address :

Email :

Home :

Work :

Phone :

Social Media :

Birthday :

ADDRESS LOG

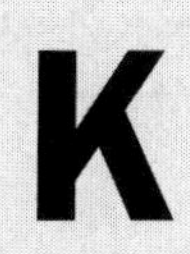

NAME :
Address :
Email :
Home :
Work :
Phone :
Social Media :
Birthday :

• •

NAME :
Address :
Email :
Home :
Work :
Phone :
Social Media :
Birthday :

• •

NAME :
Address :
Email :
ome :
Work :
Phone :
Social Media :
Birthday :

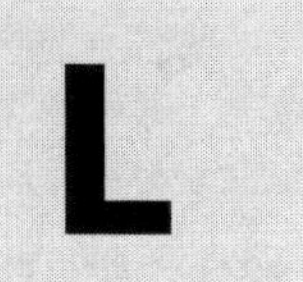

ADDRESS LOG

NAME :

Address :

Email :

Home :

Work :

Phone :

Social Media :

Birthday :

• •

NAME :

Address :

Email :

Home :

Work :

Phone :

Social Media :

Birthday :

• •

NAME :

Address :

Email :

Home :

Work :

Phone :

Social Media :

Birthday :

ADDRESS LOG

NAME :
Address :
Email :
Home :
Work :
Phone :
Social Media :
Birthday :

• •

NAME :
Address :
Email :
Home :
Work :
Phone :
Social Media :
Birthday :

• •

NAME :
Address :
Email :
Home :
Work :
Phone :
Social Media :
Birthday :

L

ADDRESS LOG

NAME :

Address :

Email :

Home :

Work :

Phone :

Social Media :

Birthday :

• •

NAME :

Address :

Email :

Home :

Work :

Phone :

Social Media :

Birthday :

• •

NAME :

Address :

Email :

Home :

Work :

Phone :

Social Media :

Birthday :

ADDRESS LOG

NAME :

Address :

Email :

Home :

Work :

Phone :

Social Media :

Birthday :

• •

NAME :

Address :

Email :

Home :

Work :

Phone :

Social Media :

Birthday :

• •

NAME :

Address :

Email :

Home :

Work :

Phone :

Social Media :

Birthday :

ADDRESS LOG

NAME : ______________________

Address : ______________________

Email : ______________________

Home : ______________________

Work : ______________________

Phone : ______________________

Social Media : ______________________

Birthday : ______________________

• •

NAME : ______________________

Address : ______________________

Email : ______________________

Home : ______________________

Work : ______________________

Phone : ______________________

Social Media : ______________________

Birthday : ______________________

• •

NAME : ______________________

Address : ______________________

Email : ______________________

Home : ______________________

Work : ______________________

Phone : ______________________

Social Media : ______________________

Birthday : ______________________

ADDRESS LOG

NAME :

Address :

Email :

Home :

Work :

Phone :

Social Media :

Birthday :

• •

NAME :

Address :

Email :

Home :

Work :

Phone :

Social Media :

Birthday :

• •

NAME :

Address :

Email :

Home :

Work :

Phone :

Social Media :

Birthday :

ADDRESS LOG

NAME :

Address :

Email :

Home :

Work :

Phone :

Social Media :

Birthday :

• •

NAME :

Address :

Email :

Home :

Work :

Phone :

Social Media :

Birthday :

• •

NAME :

Address :

Email :

Home :

Work :

Phone :

Social Media :

Birthday :

ADDRESS LOG

NAME :

Address :

Email :

Home :

Work :

Phone :

Social Media :

Birthday :

• •

NAME :

Address :

Email :

Home :

Work :

Phone :

Social Media :

Birthday :

• •

NAME :

Address :

Email :

Home :

Work :

Phone :

Social Media :

Birthday :

N

ADDRESS LOG

NAME :

Address :

Email :

Home :

Work :

Phone :

Social Media :

Birthday :

NAME :

Address :

Email :

Home :

Work :

Phone :

Social Media :

Birthday :

NAME :

Address :

Email :

Home :

Work :

Phone :

Social Media :

Birthday :

ADDRESS LOG

NAME :

Address :

Email :

Home :

Work :

Phone :

Social Media :

Birthday :

NAME :

Address :

Email :

Home :

Work :

Phone :

Social Media :

Birthday :

NAME :

Address :

Email :

Home :

Work :

Phone :

Social Media :

Birthday :

N

ADDRESS LOG

NAME :

Address :

Email :

Home :

Work :

Phone :

Social Media :

Birthday :

NAME :

Address :

Email :

Home :

Work :

Phone :

Social Media :

Birthday :

NAME :

Address :

Email :

Home :

Work :

Phone :

Social Media :

Birthday :

ADDRESS LOG

NAME :

Address :

Email :

Home :

Work :

Phone :

Social Media :

Birthday :

• •

NAME :

Address :

Email :

Home :

Work :

Phone :

Social Media :

Birthday :

• •

NAME :

Address :

Email :

Home :

Work :

Phone :

Social Media :

Birthday :

0

ADDRESS LOG

NAME : ______________________________

Address : ______________________________

Email : ______________________________

Home : ______________________________

Work : ______________________________

Phone : ______________________________

Social Media : ______________________________

Birthday : ______________________________

• •

NAME : ______________________________

Address : ______________________________

Email : ______________________________

Home : ______________________________

Work : ______________________________

Phone : ______________________________

Social Media : ______________________________

Birthday : ______________________________

• •

NAME : ______________________________

Address : ______________________________

Email : ______________________________

Home : ______________________________

Work : ______________________________

Phone : ______________________________

Social Media : ______________________________

Birthday : ______________________________

ADDRESS LOG

O

NAME :

Address :

Email :

Home :

Work :

Phone :

Social Media :

Birthday :

• •

NAME :

Address :

Email :

Home :

Work :

Phone :

Social Media :

Birthday :

• •

NAME :

Address :

Email :

Home :

Work :

Phone :

Social Media :

Birthday :

0

ADDRESS LOG

NAME :

Address :

Email :

Home :

Work :

Phone :

Social Media :

Birthday :

NAME :

Address :

Email :

Home :

Work :

Phone :

Social Media :

Birthday :

NAME :

Address :

Email :

Home :

Work :

Phone :

Social Media :

Birthday :

ADDRESS LOG

O

NAME :

Address :

Email :

Home :

Work :

Phone :

Social Media :

Birthday :

• •

NAME :

Address :

Email :

Home :

Work :

Phone :

Social Media :

Birthday :

• •

NAME :

Address :

Email :

Home :

Work :

Phone :

Social Media :

Birthday :

ADDRESS LOG

NAME :

Address :

Email :

Home :

Work :

Phone :

Social Media :

Birthday :

• •

NAME :

Address :

Email :

Home :

Work :

Phone :

Social Media :

Birthday :

• •

NAME :

Address :

Email :

Home :

Work :

Phone :

Social Media :

Birthday :

ADDRESS LOG

NAME :

Address :

Email :

Home :

Work :

Phone :

Social Media :

Birthday :

• •

NAME :

Address :

Email :

Home :

Work :

Phone :

Social Media :

Birthday :

• •

NAME :

Address :

Email :

Home :

Work :

Phone :

Social Media :

Birthday :

ADDRESS LOG

NAME :
Address :
Email :
Home :
Work :
Phone :
Social Media :
Birthday :

• •

NAME :
Address :
Email :
Home :
Work :
Phone :
Social Media :
Birthday :

• •

NAME :
Address :
Email :
Home :
Work :
Phone :
Social Media :
Birthday :

ADDRESS LOG

NAME :

Address :

Email :

Home :

Work :

Phone :

Social Media :

Birthday :

• •

NAME :

Address :

Email :

Home :

Work :

Phone :

Social Media :

Birthday :

• •

NAME :

Address :

Email :

Home :

Work :

Phone :

Social Media :

Birthday :

ADDRESS LOG

NAME :

Address :

Email :

Home :

Work :

Phone :

Social Media :

Birthday :

• •

NAME :

Address :

Email :

Home :

Work :

Phone :

Social Media :

Birthday :

• •

NAME :

Address :

Email :

Home :

Work :

Phone :

Social Media :

Birthday :

ADDRESS LOG

Q

NAME :

Address :

Email :

Home :

Work :

Phone :

Social Media :

Birthday :

• •

NAME :

Address :

Email :

Home :

Work :

Phone :

Social Media :

Birthday :

• •

NAME :

Address :

Email :

Home :

Work :

Phone :

Social Media :

Birthday :

ADDRESS LOG

NAME :
Address :
Email :
Home :
Work :
Phone :
Social Media :
Birthday :

• •

NAME :
Address :
Email :
Home :
Work :
Phone :
Social Media :
Birthday :

• •

NAME :
Address :
Email :
Home :
Work :
Phone :
Social Media :
Birthday :

ADDRESS LOG

Q

NAME :
Address :
Email :
Home :
Work :
Phone :
Social Media :
Birthday :

• •

NAME :
Address :
Email :
Home :
Work :
Phone :
Social Media :
Birthday :

• •

NAME :
Address :
Email :
Home :
Work :
Phone :
Social Media :
Birthday :

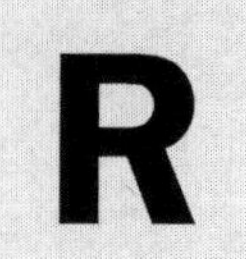

ADDRESS LOG

NAME :

Address :

Email :

Home :

Work :

Phone :

Social Media :

Birthday :

• •

NAME :

Address :

Email :

Home :

Work :

Phone :

Social Media :

Birthday :

• •

NAME :

Address :

Email :

Home :

Work :

Phone :

Social Media :

Birthday :

ADDRESS LOG

NAME :

Address :

Email :

Home :

Work :

Phone :

Social Media :

Birthday :

NAME :

Address :

Email :

Home :

Work :

Phone :

Social Media :

Birthday :

NAME :

Address :

Email :

Home :

Work :

Phone :

Social Media :

Birthday :

ADDRESS LOG

NAME :

Address :

Email :

Home :

Work :

Phone :

Social Media :

Birthday :

• •

NAME :

Address :

Email :

Home :

Work :

Phone :

Social Media :

Birthday :

• •

NAME :

Address :

Email :

Home :

Work :

Phone :

Social Media :

Birthday :

ADDRESS LOG

NAME :

Address :

Email :

Home :

Work :

Phone :

Social Media :

Birthday :

• •

NAME :

Address :

Email :

Home :

Work :

Phone :

Social Media :

Birthday :

• •

NAME :

Address :

Email :

Home :

Work :

Phone :

Social Media :

Birthday :

S

ADDRESS LOG

NAME : ________________

Address :

Email :

Home :

Work :

Phone :

Social Media :

Birthday :

• •

NAME :

Address :

Email :

Home :

Work :

Phone :

Social Media :

Birthday :

• •

NAME :

Address :

Email :

Home :

Work :

Phone :

Social Media :

Birthday :

ADDRESS LOG

S

NAME :

Address :

Email :

Home :

Work :

Phone :

Social Media :

Birthday :

• •

NAME :

Address :

Email :

Home :

Work :

Phone :

Social Media :

Birthday :

• •

NAME :

Address :

Email :

Home :

Work :

Phone :

Social Media :

Birthday :

S

ADDRESS LOG

NAME :

Address :

Email :

Home :

Work :

Phone :

Social Media :

Birthday :

• •

NAME :

Address :

Email :

Home :

Work :

Phone :

Social Media :

Birthday :

• •

NAME :

Address :

Email :

Home :

Work :

Phone :

Social Media :

Birthday :

ADDRESS LOG

S

NAME :

Address :

Email :

Home :

Work :

Phone :

Social Media :

Birthday :

• •

NAME :

Address :

Email :

Home :

Work :

Phone :

Social Media :

Birthday :

• •

NAME :

Address :

Email :

Home :

Work :

Phone :

Social Media :

Birthday :

T

ADDRESS LOG

NAME :

Address :

Email :

Home :

Work :

Phone :

Social Media :

Birthday :

• •

NAME :

Address :

Email :

Home :

Work :

Phone :

Social Media :

Birthday :

• •

NAME :

Address :

Email :

Home :

Work :

Phone :

Social Media :

Birthday :

ADDRESS LOG

T

NAME :
Address :
Email :
Home :
Work :
Phone :
Social Media :
Birthday :

NAME :
Address :
Email :
Home :
Work :
Phone :
Social Media :
Birthday :

NAME :
Address :
Email :
Home :
Work :
Phone :
Social Media :
Birthday :

T

ADDRESS LOG

NAME :

Address :

Email :

Home :

Work :

Phone :

Social Media :

Birthday :

• •

NAME :

Address :

Email :

Home :

Work :

Phone :

Social Media :

Birthday :

• •

NAME :

Address :

Email :

Home :

Work :

Phone :

Social Media :

Birthday :

ADDRESS LOG

T

NAME :

Address :

Email :

Home :

Work :

Phone :

Social Media :

Birthday :

NAME :

Address :

Email :

Home :

Work :

Phone :

Social Media :

Birthday :

NAME :

Address :

Email :

Home :

Work :

Phone :

Social Media :

Birthday :

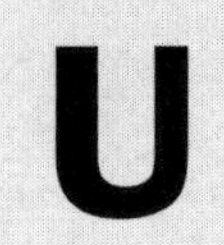

ADDRESS LOG

NAME :

Address :

Email :

Home :

Work :

Phone :

Social Media :

Birthday :

NAME :

Address :

Email :

Home :

Work :

Phone :

Social Media :

Birthday :

NAME :

Address :

Email :

Home :

Work :

Phone :

Social Media :

Birthday :

ADDRESS LOG

NAME : ______________________

Address : ______________________

Email : ______________________

Home : ______________________

Work : ______________________

Phone : ______________________

Social Media : ______________________

Birthday : ______________________

• •

NAME : ______________________

Address : ______________________

Email : ______________________

Home : ______________________

Work : ______________________

Phone : ______________________

Social Media : ______________________

Birthday : ______________________

• •

NAME : ______________________

Address : ______________________

Email : ______________________

Home : ______________________

Work : ______________________

Phone : ______________________

Social Media : ______________________

Birthday : ______________________

ADDRESS LOG

NAME :

Address :

Email :

Home :

Work :

Phone :

Social Media :

Birthday :

• •

NAME :

Address :

Email :

Home :

Work :

Phone :

Social Media :

Birthday :

• •

NAME :

Address :

Email :

Home :

Work :

Phone :

Social Media :

Birthday :

ADDRESS LOG

NAME :

Address :

Email :

Home :

Work :

Phone :

Social Media :

Birthday :

• •

NAME :

Address :

Email :

Home :

Work :

Phone :

Social Media :

Birthday :

• •

NAME :

Address :

Email :

Home :

Work :

Phone :

Social Media :

Birthday :

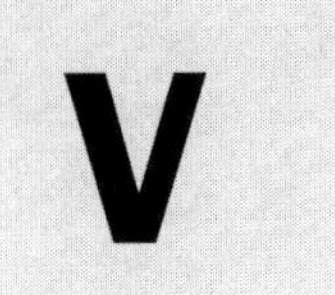

ADDRESS LOG

NAME : ______________________

Address : ______________________

Email : ______________________

Home : ______________________

Work : ______________________

Phone : ______________________

Social Media : ______________________

Birthday : ______________________

• •

NAME : ______________________

Address : ______________________

Email : ______________________

Home : ______________________

Work : ______________________

Phone : ______________________

Social Media : ______________________

Birthday : ______________________

• •

NAME : ______________________

Address : ______________________

Email : ______________________

Home : ______________________

Work : ______________________

Phone : ______________________

Social Media : ______________________

Birthday : ______________________

ADDRESS LOG

NAME :

Address :

Email :

Home :

Work :

Phone :

Social Media :

Birthday :

• •

NAME :

Address :

Email :

Home :

Work :

Phone :

Social Media :

Birthday :

• •

NAME :

Address :

Email :

Home :

Work :

Phone :

Social Media :

Birthday :

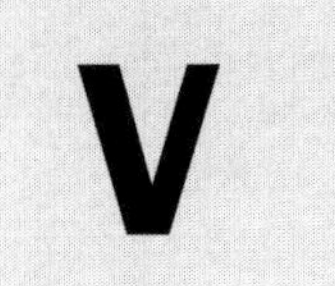

ADDRESS LOG

NAME :

Address :

Email :

Home :

Work :

Phone :

Social Media :

Birthday :

NAME :

Address :

Email :

Home :

Work :

Phone :

Social Media :

Birthday :

NAME :

Address :

Email :

Home :

Work :

Phone :

Social Media :

Birthday :

ADDRESS LOG

NAME :

Address :

Email :

Home :

Work :

Phone :

Social Media :

Birthday :

• •

NAME :

Address :

Email :

Home :

Work :

Phone :

Social Media :

Birthday :

• •

NAME :

Address :

Email :

Home :

Work :

Phone :

Social Media :

Birthday :

ADDRESS LOG

NAME : ______________________

Address : ______________________

Email : ______________________

Home : ______________________

Work : ______________________

Phone : ______________________

Social Media : ______________________

Birthday : ______________________

• •

NAME : ______________________

Address : ______________________

Email : ______________________

Home : ______________________

Work : ______________________

Phone : ______________________

Social Media : ______________________

Birthday : ______________________

• •

NAME : ______________________

Address : ______________________

Email : ______________________

Home : ______________________

Work : ______________________

Phone : ______________________

Social Media : ______________________

Birthday : ______________________

ADDRESS LOG

NAME :

Address :

Email :

Home :

Work :

Phone :

Social Media :

Birthday :

• •

NAME :

Address :

Email :

Home :

Work :

Phone :

Social Media :

Birthday :

• •

NAME :

Address :

Email :

Home :

Work :

Phone :

Social Media :

Birthday :

ADDRESS LOG

NAME : ______________________________

Address : ______________________________

Email : ______________________________

Home : ______________________________

Work : ______________________________

Phone : ______________________________

Social Media : ______________________________

Birthday : ______________________________

• •

NAME : ______________________________

Address : ______________________________

Email : ______________________________

Home : ______________________________

Work : ______________________________

Phone : ______________________________

Social Media : ______________________________

Birthday : ______________________________

• •

NAME : ______________________________

Address : ______________________________

Email : ______________________________

Home : ______________________________

Work : ______________________________

Phone : ______________________________

Social Media : ______________________________

Birthday : ______________________________

ADDRESS LOG

NAME :

Address :

Email :

Home :

Work :

Phone :

Social Media :

Birthday :

NAME :

Address :

Email :

Home :

Work :

Phone :

Social Media :

Birthday :

NAME :

Address :

Email :

Home :

Work :

Phone :

Social Media :

Birthday :

ADDRESS LOG

NAME :

Address :

Email :

Home :

Work :

Phone :

Social Media :

Birthday :

• •

NAME :

Address :

Email :

Home :

Work :

Phone :

Social Media :

Birthday :

• •

NAME :

Address :

Email :

Home :

Work :

Phone :

Social Media :

Birthday :

ADDRESS LOG

NAME :

Address :

Email :

Home :

Work :

Phone :

Social Media :

Birthday :

• •

NAME :

Address :

Email :

Home :

Work :

Phone :

Social Media :

Birthday :

• •

NAME :

Address :

Email :

Home :

Work :

Phone :

Social Media :

Birthday :

ADDRESS LOG

NAME :

Address :

Email :

Home :

Work :

Phone :

Social Media :

Birthday :

• •

NAME :

Address :

Email :

Home :

Work :

Phone :

Social Media :

Birthday :

• •

NAME :

Address :

Email :

Home :

Work :

Phone :

Social Media :

Birthday :

ADDRESS LOG

NAME :
Address :
Email :
Home :
Work :
Phone :
Social Media :
Birthday :

• •

NAME :
Address :
Email :
Home :
Work :
Phone :
Social Media :
Birthday :

• •

NAME :
Address :
Email :
Home :
Work :
Phone :
Social Media :
Birthday :

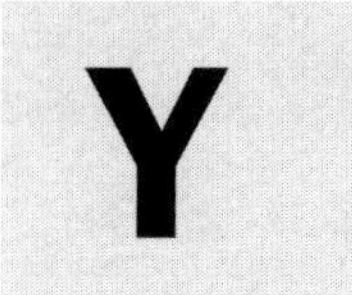

ADDRESS LOG

NAME :

Address :

Email :

Home :

Work :

Phone :

Social Media :

Birthday :

• •

NAME :

Address :

Email :

Home :

Work :

Phone :

Social Media :

Birthday :

• •

NAME :

Address :

Email :

Home :

Work :

Phone :

Social Media :

Birthday :

ADDRESS LOG

NAME :

Address :

Email :

Home :

Work :

Phone :

Social Media :

Birthday :

• •

NAME :

Address :

Email :

Home :

Work :

Phone :

Social Media :

Birthday :

• •

NAME :

Address :

Email :

Home :

Work :

Phone :

Social Media :

Birthday :

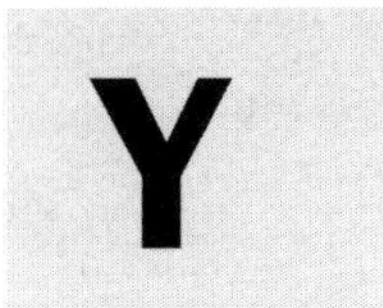

ADDRESS LOG

NAME :

Address :

Email :

Home :

Work :

Phone :

Social Media :

Birthday :

• •

NAME :

Address :

Email :

Home :

Work :

Phone :

Social Media :

Birthday :

• •

NAME :

Address :

Email :

Home :

Work :

Phone :

Social Media :

Birthday :

ADDRESS LOG

NAME :

Address :

Email :

Home :

Work :

Phone :

Social Media :

Birthday :

NAME :

Address :

Email :

Home :

Work :

Phone :

Social Media :

Birthday :

NAME :

Address :

Email :

Home :

Work :

Phone :

Social Media :

Birthday :

Z

ADDRESS LOG

NAME : ____________________

Address :

Email :

Home :

Work :

Phone :

Social Media :

Birthday :

• •

NAME : ____________________

Address :

Email :

Home :

Work :

Phone :

Social Media :

Birthday :

• •

NAME : ____________________

Address :

Email :

Home :

Work :

Phone :

Social Media :

Birthday :

ADDRESS LOG

Z

NAME :
Address :
Email :
Home :
Work :
Phone :
Social Media :
Birthday :

• •

NAME :
Address :
Email :
Home :
Work :
Phone :
Social Media :
Birthday :

• •

NAME :
Address :
Email :
Home :
Work :
Phone :
Social Media :
Birthday :

Z

ADDRESS LOG

NAME :

Address :

Email :

Home :

Work :

Phone :

Social Media :

Birthday :

• •

NAME :

Address :

Email :

Home :

Work :

Phone :

Social Media :

Birthday :

• •

NAME :

Address :

Email :

Home :

Work :

Phone :

Social Media :

Birthday :

ADDRESS LOG

Z

NAME :

Address :

Email :

Home :

Work :

Phone :

Social Media :

Birthday :

• •

NAME :

Address :

Email :

Home :

Work :

Phone :

Social Media :

Birthday :

• •

NAME :

Address :

Email :

Home :

Work :

Phone :

Social Media :

Birthday :

Made in the USA
Middletown, DE
19 July 2022